MATRIX REIMPRINTING

Unlocking Your Potential, A Step-By-Step Approach To Harnessing The Power Of Self-Discovery And Emotional Well-Being

CW00498324

DR. WANDA MENDENHALL

DISCLAIMER

This book is the result of the author's own expertise, insight, and experience in the area of treatment. The author has no affiliation with any particular firm, business, or person mentioned in this article. The content in this book is based exclusively on the author's knowledge and should not be construed as professional advice or a replacement for professional treatment or counseling.

Readers are recommended to seek professional counsel or guidance based on their unique circumstances or requirements. The author and publisher are not liable for any actions done in reliance on the information included in this book. Every person's circumstance is unique, so what works for one person may not work for another.

This book attempts to provide insights and knowledge for both education and personal growth.

The author does not recommend any certain therapy strategy or practice over another. Readers should exercise caution and check with trained specialists before using any knowledge or strategies discussed in this book.

By reading this book, the reader understands and accepts that the author and publisher are not accountable for any direct or indirect repercussions, damages, or losses that occur from the use or misuse of the material included herein.

Table of Contents

INTRODUCTION

Welcome to the life-changing realm of Matrix Reimprinting! This ground-breaking technique combines cutting-edge psychology and energy work to unleash your mind's enormous capacity to transform your world.

Welcoming You To Matrix Reimprinting

Matrix Reimprinting is more than a therapy procedure; it's a trip into the depths of your awareness that provides a unique insight into how your previous experiences impact your present and future. Karl Dawson created it as an extension of the ideas of the Emotional

Freedom Technique (EFT) to produce a powerful instrument for personal development and healing.

Understanding The Power Of The Mind

The belief in the extraordinary power of the mind is at the heart of Matrix Reimprinting. It is based on the idea that our experiences, particularly those from infancy, leave impressions or matrixes on our minds, emotions, and actions. These impressions serve as the lens through which we view and interact with our surroundings.

Exploring The Origins Of Matrix Reimprinting

Matrix Reimprinting stems from the realization that unresolved bad events may get entrenched in our energy system, negatively harming our well-being. This approach allows us to reimprint these memories with more powerful thoughts and feelings by revisiting these events inside the matrix of our brains.

The technique combines components of quantum physics, neurology, and psychology, acknowledging the interdependence of mind, body, and energy. It operates on the concept that by changing the perception and emotional charge linked to previous events, we may drastically influence our current reality and future experiences.

Matrix Reimprinting allows significant healing via a mix of vision, communication, and energy adjustments. It enables people to have access to the subconscious mind, which contains many of our beliefs and emotional patterns and creates big beneficial changes.

Matrix Reimprinting is essentially about empowerment, providing a platform for self-discovery, healing, and personal development. Individuals may break free from limiting ideas, release emotional loads, and create a more meaningful present and future by reviewing and reframing previous events in a safe and supportive atmosphere.

In the parts that follow, we'll go further into the ideas and practices behind Matrix Reimprinting, examining its applications, advantages, and transformational potential for individuals seeking holistic treatment and personal development.

CHAPTER ONE

Foundations Of Matrix Reimprinting

Unveiling The Core Principles

Karl Dawson's transformational psychological approach, Matrix Reimprinting, is based on three essential ideas that support its success in resolving emotional issues:

1. Matrix - Understanding the Energy Matrix: The notion that our experiences are energetically stored in a matrix—a web-like network inside us—where prior memories, beliefs, and emotions interact is central to Matrix Reimprinting.

This matrix has an impact on our current experiences and perspectives.

2. Matrix Reimprinting draws on notions from quantum physics to propose that every instant occurs simultaneously inside this matrix. Changing our perspective of previous events may have an impact on the present and future, similar to the concept of non-linear time.

3. **Memory Reconsolidation Theory:** Matrix Reimprinting corresponds to the memory reconsolidation theory in psychology, which proposes that our memories are not fixed but may be reprocessed and rewritten, allowing for the modification of related emotions and ideas.

4. It focuses on empowering people to modify their experiences by adjusting views on previous events, allowing them to remove harmful emotions and beliefs contained inside the matrix.

Recognizing The Connection To EFT (Emotional Freedom Technique)

Matrix Reimprinting is closely related to EFT, or Emotional Freedom Technique, a well-known technique that involves tapping on precise meridian points. Matrix Reimprinting, on the other hand, extends EFT by including numerous additional components:

1. Matrix Reimprinting uses the concepts of EFT as a foundation by merging

tapping with the matrix reimprinting method. Tapping aids in the retrieval and release of stored emotions associated with particular memories inside the matrix.

2. Using Imagery and Visualization to Address Core Issues: While EFT generally focuses on tapping to relieve emotional distress, Matrix Reimprinting goes further by employing visualization and imagery methods to engage with and reimprint the matrix.

3. Matrix Reimprinting, unlike EFT, includes communicating with previous selves or 'echoes' inside the matrix, promoting discussion and resolution of traumatic or upsetting memories. This

enables substantial healing and reframement of prior events.

Embracing The Matrix Reimprinting Philosophy

The Matrix Reimprinting concept includes a comprehensive approach to healing and personal development:

1. **Mind-Body Connection:** It recognizes the delicate relationship between the mind and body, realizing that emotional experiences influence both mental and physical health.

2. **Empowerment and Self-Agency:** The focus of Matrix Reimprinting is on enabling people to take an active part in their recovery path.

It fosters a feeling of self-agency and empowerment by offering tools for rewriting their narratives.

3. Compassionate Transformation: The ideology promotes compassion and awareness of oneself and one's surroundings. It acknowledges that people may build more compassionate relationships and a better self-image by healing previous wounds and releasing bad emotions.

4. Unleashing Potential via Resilience: Matrix Reimprinting attempts to reveal an individual's inner resilience and potential by changing previous events, allowing them to build a more meaningful and powerful present and future.

CHAPTER TWO

The Inner Workings Of Matrix Reimprinting

Mapping The Landscape Of The Matrix

Matrix Reimprinting dives into the complexities of our inner world, probing the matrix of our consciousness—a storehouse of memories, beliefs, and experiences. This environment isn't simply a static archive; it's a living web where previous events and current emotions collide, changing our perceptions and reactions. In this chapter, we travel the matrix, learning about its landscape and how it affects our experience.

The matrix is a holographic tapestry in which memories live in a multidimensional realm, influencing our thoughts, emotions, and actions. Practitioners lead people via Matrix Reimprinting to access this matrix, enabling them to reframe, heal, and transcend previous events, consequently transforming their current condition.

Embracing The Role Of Memories And Beliefs

Memories are imprints in our awareness that dictate how we respond to comparable experiences. They are more than simply memories; they are emotional imprints that shape our views, often unknowingly.

Matrix Reimprinting recognizes the importance of memories in forming our ideas and actions and recognizes that unresolved unpleasant experiences may perpetuate patterns of suffering or constraint.

These memories provide substance to our beliefs, which are like threads sewn into the fabric of our lives. They become lenses through which we see the world. Matrix Reimprinting encourages us to investigate these ideas and trace them back to their source inside the matrix. Individuals gain a significant chance for healing and progress by acknowledging and reframing these ideas rooted in prior experiences.

Grasping The Mechanics Of Transformative Visualization

Within Matrix Reimprinting, visualization serves as a link between the conscious and subconscious worlds. Individuals are enabled to revisit prior memories as active participants rather than passive spectators using guided procedures. This transformational visualization method includes conversing with the younger self-present in the recollection, giving comfort, direction, and the chance to re-write the experience.

Individuals may intentionally rewire their subconscious reactions by bringing fresh views, emotions, or resolves into these memories. This visualization's mechanics require not just a cerebral reviewing, but also an emotional and energy reconfiguration. It's a method that delves into memory's malleability, allowing for tremendous healing and empowerment.

Finally, Matrix Reimprinting is a revolutionary way to understand and modify the mind's inner environment. Individuals go on a path of healing, self-discovery, and significant personal transformation by traversing the matrix, confronting memories and beliefs, and using transformative imagery.

CHAPTER THREE

Navigating Techniques And Practices

Matrix Reimprinting is a potent technique for reshaping perceptions and transforming previous experiences. In this chapter, we'll go over a step-by-step approach to Matrix Reimprinting, as well as the tools and techniques for running productive sessions and overcoming problems in practice.

Step-By-Step Guide To Matrix Reimprinting

1. Preparation and Intention Setting: Begin by setting a safe and comfortable environment for the session. Set clear objectives for what you want to accomplish throughout the session, whether it's addressing a particular problem, releasing trauma, or boosting self-esteem.

2. Identifying the Target Memory: Assist the client in recalling a particular upsetting memory. This memory is the portal into the matrix, the energetic field in which all events are recorded.

3. Entering the Matrix: The practitioner assists the client in entering the memory by using visualization and tapping methods. Accessing the emotions, experiences, and beliefs related to that event is required.

4. Using the ECHO: The ECHO (Energetic Consciousness Hologram) is a memory representation of the client's younger self. Interact with the ECHO to build rapport and grasp their point of view.

5. Empowering approaches: Use a variety of approaches inside the matrix to aid healing. This might include discourse, reframing, visualization, or even inserting supporting individuals to favorably influence the memory's narrative.

6. Reimprinting: Rewriting the memory's script by adding fresh viewpoints, resources, and resolves is a critical step. Encourage the client to actively reinterpret the experience to change it into a more powerful story.

7. Integration and Closure: Help the client exit the matrix by making them feel grounded and focused. Discuss discoveries and support good changes in thoughts and emotions.

Tools And Methods For Effective Sessions

1. Tapping: To relieve emotional barriers and enable transformation inside the matrix, use Emotional Freedom Techniques (EFT) or tapping on particular acupressure sites.

2. Visualization: Guide the customer via colorful representations to efficiently access and manage the matrix. Encourage them to use all of their senses to improve the experience.

3. Discussion Techniques: Use effective inquiry and compassionate discussion to elicit deeper levels of memories and promote ECHO change.

4. Resource Integration: To empower the client, include supporting aspects such as affirmations, strengths, and positive images into the reimprinting process.

Overcoming Challenges In Practice

1. Respecting the Client's Pace: Everyone reacts differently to the process. Respect their speed and willingness to go into difficult recollections. Progress is progress, no matter how slow it is.

2. Managing Intensity: Some memories may elicit strong emotions. Maintain a secure setting and have mechanisms in place to deal with emotional discomfort, such as grounding exercises or session breaks.

3. Managing Resistance: Clients may fight the procedure out of fear or mistrust. To handle opposition progressively, build trust, communicate effectively, and validate their feelings.

4. Continuous Learning and Supervision: Updating skills via training regularly, and seeking supervision or peer help when dealing with complicated issues or uncertainty.

Matrix Reimprinting is a transformational process that allows people to rewrite their stories and achieve positive change. Mastering its procedures and overcoming obstacles may completely release its healing and growing potential.

CHAPTER FOUR

Healing Through Matrix Reimprinting

Matrix Reimprinting is a powerful energy psychology method that allows people to confront deep-seated traumas, transcend limiting beliefs, and aid emotional recovery. This novel method is based on the idea that our previous experiences leave energy imprints that influence our current actions, emotions, and beliefs. Matrix Reimprinting leverages the potential for emotional healing by changing these imprints in Chapter Four.

Harnessing The Potential For Emotional Healing

The principle at the heart of Matrix Reimprinting is that our subconscious mind retains memories like snapshots, capturing not just the experiences but also the accompanying emotions and beliefs. These imprints, particularly those associated with traumatic events or unfavorable attitudes developed in the past, may have a substantial influence on our current experiences and emotions.

This chapter looks at how Matrix Reimprinting enables people to retrieve their stored memories in a secure and regulated setting. Individuals may successfully adjust their emotional reactions and perceptions about previous events by delving into these memories and changing their energy imprints. This approach gives people the ability to rewrite their stories, resulting in deep emotional healing and personal development.

Addressing Trauma And Limiting Beliefs

Trauma, whether major or little, often leaves an indelible mark on our minds. Matrix Reimprinting offers a novel approach to addressing and processing these experiences. Individuals might get a new perspective on their former experiences by revisiting them in a friendly and supervised setting. Traumatic imprints may be eased via strategies like as visualization, reframing, and tapping inner resources, enabling healing to occur.

Furthermore, limiting beliefs, which are often formed after difficult or traumatic experiences, may stifle personal progress and satisfaction. Individuals may use Matrix Reimprinting to uncover and convert limiting beliefs into empowered ones. Individuals may break free from the shackles of self-imposed limits by revisiting the times when these ideas were formed and reframing them with fresh viewpoints and positive affirmations.

Case Studies Illustrating Transformational Journeys

This chapter contains powerful case examples that demonstrate Matrix Reimprinting's transforming impact. These real-life examples demonstrate people who have experienced considerable emotional healing and personal progress as a result of this practice.

A case study, for example, may show how a person suffering from severe self-doubt traced it back to a childhood trauma. They revisited that moment, reframed their views, and experienced a remarkable transformation in self-confidence, allowing them to pursue their objectives with renewed vigor.

CHAPTER FIVE

Integrating Matrix Reimprinting Into Daily Life

Matrix Reimprinting, a powerful and transformational method based on quantum mechanics and EFT (Emotional Freedom Techniques), has an influence that goes well beyond the bounds of treatment sessions.

In this chapter, we look at how Matrix Reimprinting may be smoothly incorporated into everyday life, looking at how it can be used to enhance relationships, stimulate self-discovery, and promote emotional well-being and resilience.

Applying Matrix Reimprinting Beyond Sessions

1. Matrix Reimprinting Practices daily:

Matrix Reimprinting is not only for formal therapeutic sessions. Individuals may implement everyday routines to get the advantages of the strategy. Mindfulness, journaling, and self-reflection activities are examples of such techniques. Individuals may proactively address previous traumas and alter their reactions to present obstacles by participating in the Matrix Reimprinting process continuously.

2. Self-Help Tools that Empower:

Matrix Reimprinting gives people a range of powerful self-help skills.

These tools allow you to negotiate situations of tension, worry, or self-doubt on your own. Techniques like "ECHO Tapping" allow people to tap into the Matrix in real time, breaking negative thinking patterns and cultivating a more optimistic mentality.

3. Timeline Modification:

Incorporating Matrix Reimprinting into one's chronology allows for a fundamental change in vision. Individuals may impact their current and future experiences by revisiting and modifying crucial situations in their history. This notion is fundamental in everyday life since it fosters a feeling of agency and control over one's story.

Strengthening Relationships And Self-Discovery

1. Reimprinting the Relationship Matrix:

Matrix Reimprinting may help with relationship mending and enhancement. Individuals may remove emotional baggage, forgive previous grievances, and create stronger connections by analyzing and reimprinting major events within the framework of relationships. This procedure promotes a more positive emotional environment for all those involved.

2. Matrix Reimprinting for Self-Discovery:

Matrix Reimprinting is a very effective method for self-discovery.

Individuals get insights about their ideas, habits, and patterns by revisiting crucial times in their past. This increased self-awareness enables people to make conscious decisions that are in line with their real selves, resulting in personal development and satisfaction.

3. Empathy and Compassion Development:

Matrix Reimprinting promotes a sympathetic investigation of other people's experiences inside the matrix. This increased empathy leads to better communication and understanding in relationships. Individuals grow more capable of assisting others on their recovery journeys as they shed their emotional loads.

Cultivating Resilience And Emotional Well-Being

1. Reimprinting of the Resilience Matrix:

Matrix Reimprinting works as a resilience-building technique by changing how people perceive and react to situations. Individuals create a resilient attitude by reviewing prior failures and reframing them via the Matrix perspective. This transformation equips individuals to face hardship with ingenuity and agility.

2. Emotional Control and Well-Being:

Matrix Reimprinting is very beneficial in fostering emotional well-being. Individuals may use the approach to process and release pent-up emotions, avoiding the building of emotional baggage. Regular practice improves emotional control, resulting in a more balanced and harmonious interior environment.

3. The Mind-Body Connection

Matrix Reimprinting relies heavily on the mind-body link. Individuals might enjoy physical and emotional healing by treating emotional imprints stored in the body's energy system. This all-encompassing strategy promotes general well-being by instilling a feeling of vibrancy and harmony.

Finally, incorporating Matrix Reimprinting into everyday life broadens its transformational potential well beyond the treatment room. Individuals may lay the groundwork for long-term positive transformation and personal development by applying Matrix Reimprinting concepts to relationships, self-discovery, resilience building, and emotional well-being. This chapter serves as a guide for incorporating the magic of Matrix Reimprinting into the fabric of daily life.

CHAPTER SIX

Advancing Skills And Mastery

In the world of Matrix Reimprinting, Chapter Six represents a watershed moment in practitioners' travels, encompassing the critical stage of increasing abilities and mastering the art of this transforming process. This chapter serves as a guide for anyone looking to expand their knowledge, develop their practice, and improve their Matrix Reimprinting skills.

Deepening Your Understanding Of Matrix Reimprinting

Practitioners at this level dive into the intricate layers of Matrix Reimprinting, developing their understanding beyond the core concepts. Immersion in the theoretical foundations that support this strategy is required for deeper comprehension. This involves reviewing core principles from quantum physics, neuroscience, and the mind-body connection—essential foundations underpinning the effectiveness of Matrix Reimprinting.

In addition, practitioners investigate the complex dynamics of trauma, subconscious patterning, and the impact of memory reconsolidation. Understanding how these aspects interact inside the matrix enables practitioners to better navigate their customers' experiences. They learn to recognize tiny indications and patterns within the matrix, allowing them to intervene with more precision and effect.

Enhancing Intuition And Connection

In Chapter Six, practitioners harness and increase their intuitive abilities, which is a key distinction between adept and proficient practitioners. This entails building a stronger connection with one's intuition as well as the capacity to sense and comprehend energy clues inside the matrix. This enhanced intuition allows practitioners to have a deeper knowledge of their client's needs, allowing them to more effectively lead them through transforming experiences.

Furthermore, practitioners improve their sympathetic abilities, promoting a stronger emotional and energetic connection with clients. This empathic resonance inside the matrix offers a secure and trusting setting, which is critical for supporting significant healing and change.

Honing Your Practice For Maximum Impact

Matrix Reimprinting mastery requires ongoing refining and polishing of one's technique. Practitioners investigate various tactics, tools, and approaches to improve their interventions and ensure maximum effect and efficacy. This involves incorporating complementary therapies into their arsenal, such as EFT

(Emotional Freedom methods), mindfulness practices, visualization methods, and somatic experience.

Practitioners also emphasize personal growth and self-care. Recognizing that their state of being has a significant impact on the matrix, they emphasize having a balanced and grounded presence. This self-awareness allows practitioners to approach sessions with more clarity, compassion, and honesty, boosting their efficacy in enabling transformational experiences.

Finally, Chapter Six is a watershed moment in the Matrix Reimprinting practitioner's path. It is a chapter about expanding understanding, amplifying intuition, and refining practice—an important step toward mastery and having the greatest influence in helping people through significant healing and change inside their matrices.

CHAPTER SEVEN

Matrix Reimprinting Across Different Contexts

Matrix Reimprinting is a strong method that transcends particular settings, making it usable in a variety of fields including health, business, and personal development. This chapter dives into the adaptability of Matrix Reimprinting, investigating its usefulness in a variety of environments and how it may be adjusted to meet a variety of demands.

Utilizing Matrix Reimprinting In Various Settings

The versatility of Matrix Reimprinting is what makes it so appealing. It's a strategy based on the realization that our previous experiences impact our current reality. Matrix Reimprinting, whether used in therapeutic settings, corporate coaching, or personal development programs, provides a powerful technique to confront underlying beliefs and traumas.

Practitioners use Matrix Reimprinting in therapy to work with clients on prior traumatic events. Individuals may shed emotional baggage and reframe their viewpoints by revisiting these experiences in a safe setting and changing their perceptions. This method promotes resilience and a revitalized sense of self while allowing for significant healing without re-traumatization.

Furthermore, in the field of business and professional coaching, Matrix Reimprinting is used to identify and reshape limiting beliefs that impede achievement. This strategy may help entrepreneurs and professionals who are tormented by self-doubt, fear of failure, or prior disappointments rewire their mental frames. Individuals may improve their performance and attain their objectives by imprinting powerful thoughts and images.

Applications In Health, Business, And Personal Growth

Matrix Reimprinting enhances standard medical techniques in the realm of health by addressing the emotional and psychological origins of disorders.

It helps people comprehend the mind-body link and allows them to work through emotional obstacles that may lead to physical problems. Individuals often report increases in their general well-being after altering their perspectives of prior traumatic experiences or ongoing pressures.

By empowering workers, Matrix Reimprinting develops a healthy organizational culture in commercial environments. Addressing workplace stresses or prior unpleasant experiences may boost employee morale and productivity dramatically. Leaders may also benefit from Matrix Reimprinting procedures to improve their leadership abilities and decision-making processes.

Matrix Reimprinting is a catalyst for change on a personal level. This strategy permits people to rewrite their narratives, whether it's conquering phobias, enhancing self-esteem, or breaking away from self-sabotaging routines. People may build a more empowered present and future for themselves by examining and reworking previous occurrences.

Tailoring Approaches For Diverse Needs

One of Matrix Reimprinting's benefits is its versatility to a variety of demands. Therapists, coaches, and practitioners may adjust their approach to their clients' or participants' individual needs. This may include incorporating different therapy methods, changing the tempo of the sessions, or tailoring the methodology to cultural or individual preferences.

In a therapeutic environment, for example, practitioners may combine Matrix Reimprinting with treatments such as EMDR (Eye Movement Desensitization and Reprocessing) or cognitive-behavioral therapy to increase its efficacy for certain people. Similarly, the use of business coaching may differ depending on the nature of the sector, the issues encountered by professionals, and the corporate culture.

Finally, Matrix Reimprinting is a dynamic and revolutionary process that crosses borders. Its versatility and capacity for substantial transformation are shown by its success in a variety of situations, ranging from treatments to business coaching and personal development. Tailoring the method to match the requirements of people and communities enables for a more customized and meaningful application, enabling healing, development, and empowerment.

CHAPTER EIGHT

Ethics And Responsibility In Matrix Reimprinting

Matrix Reimprinting, a novel methodology in the field of energy psychology, presents a revolutionary mechanism for reprogramming previous experiences. As practitioners use this powerful approach, they must manage ethical issues, maintain professionalism, and accept responsibility for assisting client development.

Exploring Ethical Considerations

Any therapeutic or transformational activity is built on ethics. Several ethical considerations are important in Matrix Reimprinting:

1. Informed Consent: Practitioners must ensure that clients completely understand the technique, its ramifications, and its results before participating in Matrix Reimprinting sessions. Informed consent is critical for enabling people to make informed decisions regarding their involvement.

2. Client confidentiality must be respected at all times. Unless clear permission or legal responsibilities require disclosure, practitioners must preserve complete confidentiality about client information, experiences, and session content.

3. Respecting Autonomy: During the therapy process, clients should have agency and autonomy.

Practitioners must respect their clients' choices, opinions, and decisions, and they must abstain from imposing personal ideas or agendas during sessions.

4. **Cultural Sensitivity and Diversity:** It is important to embrace cultural diversity and understand how diverse backgrounds impact experiences. Practitioners must be aware of cultural subtleties, avoid making assumptions, and appreciate the diversity of each client's culture.

Maintaining Professionalism And Boundaries

Matrix Reimprinting necessitates a high degree of professionalism as well as the observance of ethical boundaries:

1. Continuous Education and Training: Matrix Reimprinting practitioners must keep current on the newest advances, methodologies, and ethical norms. Continuous learning fosters proficiency and ethical behavior.

2. Boundary Management: It is critical to have clear boundaries between the practitioner and the client. This includes avoiding parallel relationships, and conflicts of interest, and maintaining professional behavior both in and out of sessions.

3. Regular self-reflection and seeking supervision or peer consultation assist practitioners in remaining aware of their biases, triggers, and personal limits that may impact their profession.

Responsibility In Facilitating Transformation

Practitioners have a lot of duty when it comes to supporting clients through their transformative journey:

1. Client Empowerment without Dependence: The goal is to empower customers rather than generate reliance. Practitioners should foster self-reliance and self-discovery, as well as provide clients with skills to help them negotiate their experiences outside of sessions.

2. Safety and Well-Being: It is critical to prioritize clients' safety and emotional well-being. Practitioners must provide a secure environment in which clients may

explore and process their feelings without feeling overwhelmed or uncomfortable.

3. Recognizing the limits of Matrix Reimprinting, practitioners should understand when a client may benefit from other types of treatment or professional assistance. For complete treatment, collaboration, and referral to additional experts may be required.

Finally, Chapter Eight emphasizes the ethical duties and professional behavior necessary in Matrix Reimprinting. Practitioners are critical in fostering transformational experiences while adhering to ethical norms, respecting boundaries, and assuring their clients' well-being during the process.

Conclusion

Reflecting On Your Matrix Reimprinting Journey

Matrix Reimprinting is reliving previous experiences via a holistic viewpoint. It is about realizing that our subconscious retains unresolved emotions and beliefs from earlier events, which influence our current behavior and decisions. Individuals investigate these subconscious imprints throughout the trip, frequently revealing the fundamental reasons for limiting beliefs or emotional patterns.

The procedure provides for a significant change in viewpoint.

Individuals may change the emotional charge connected with these memories by revisiting them from a more powerful perspective. It is not about altering the past, but rather reframing it to encourage healing and empowerment. You may notice substantial adjustments in how you view yourself and your life as you reflect on your Matrix Reimprinting adventure.

Empowering Yourself And Others

Matrix Reimprinting is a method for encouraging development and healing in others, not simply personal empowerment. Practitioners may help clients reinvent their narratives and alter their lives by learning how their prior experiences impact their ideas and actions.

The empowerment comes from realizing that we are not victims of our circumstances, but rather makers of our reality. We get the ability to rewrite our tales, release old traumas, and incorporate new, empowered beliefs by tapping into the matrix of our history. This empowerment spreads, influencing not just people but whole communities as they embrace their ability to effect good change.

Embracing The Transformative Potential Of Matrix Reimprinting

Matrix Reimprinting's revolutionary potential stems from its capacity to bridge the gap between our past, present, and future selves. It's about admitting that our views of previous events often impact our current circumstances. We open ourselves up to new possibilities and potentials by reworking these views.

Individuals may experience substantial adjustments in numerous parts of their lives, from relationships and job pathways to health and self-esteem, using this strategy. Matrix Reimprinting becomes a catalyst for personal and communal change as more individuals embrace its transformational potential.

To summarize, Matrix Reimprinting is more than simply a therapeutic tool; it is a paradigm revolution. It challenges us to rethink the narratives we tell ourselves about our history, present, and future. We can access our intrinsic power to heal, develop, and create the lives we want by adopting this approach.

THE END